This book belongs to:

....

Copyright © BPA Publishing Ltd 2020

Author: Pip Reid
Illustrator: Thomas Barnett
Creative Director: Curtis Reid

www.biblepathwayadventures.com

Thank you for supporting Bible Pathway Adventures®. Our adventure series helps parents teach their children more about the Bible in a fun creative way. Designed for the whole family, Bible Pathway Adventures' mission is to help bring discipleship back into homes around the world. The search for truth is more fun than tradition!

The moral rights of author and illustrator have been asserted, this book is copyright.

ISBN: 978-0-473-39816-3

Escape from Egypt

Moses and the Ten Plagues

"God said, 'I have seen how my people are being oppressed in Egypt and heard their cry...'"
(Exodus 3:7)

When the Hebrew people first came to Egypt, they had an easy life. Joseph, son of their leader Jacob, was a good friend of the Pharaoh. But after he died, other Pharaohs who didn't like the Hebrews began to rule the land. The Pharaohs made the Hebrews work harder and harder, and they cried out to Yahweh, the God of Abraham, Isaac, and Jacob, to save them.

"God, please don't forget your people. Save us from this evil Pharaoh!"

Even though it didn't seem like it, God had everything figured out. He hadn't forgotten His promise with Abraham to make the Hebrew people a great nation. Although God allowed them to be taken into slavery, He also had a plan to free them. His plan included a baby called Moses, who would one day grow up to lead the Hebrew people out of Egypt.

Did you know?

Many people believe there are different ways to pronounce God's name. These include Yah, Yahweh, Yahuah, and many others.

Moses was born at a time when Pharaoh was killing the Hebrew children. There were more Hebrews than Egyptians, and Pharaoh was scared that one day the Hebrew children would grow up and join his enemies.

"The Hebrews have too many children," Pharaoh told the midwives. "If a Hebrew woman gives birth to a boy, kill him. If it's a girl, let her live."

Moses' mother heard about Pharaoh's new law. *Pharaoh will not take my son*, she thought. Before Pharaoh's men could find her baby boy, she came up with a clever plan. To save Moses' life, she laid him in a woven basket and placed him in the reeds by the Nile River.

While Pharaoh's daughter bathed in the Nile a little later that day, she spotted a baby in a basket by the riverbank. "This must be one of the Hebrew children," she said. She gazed at the baby boy. "He's very cute. Maybe I should keep him."

Moses' sister, Miriam, was watching behind the reeds to see what would happen to her brother. She rushed out from where she had been hiding. "Princess, shall I find you a Hebrew woman to nurse the baby?"

Miriam ran to fetch her mother, who was the perfect woman to take care of Moses. Pharaoh's daughter was happy to have a Hebrew woman take care of the baby. When Moses was a little older, his mother took him back to live with the princess.

Did you know?

Moses' name means 'to draw out' because he was drawn out of the water.

Moses grew up in the royal palace as Pharaoh's grandson. He wore the finest clothes, ate the best food, and learned from the smartest teachers. Servants bowed down to him, and Egyptian men were afraid of him.

Life was more fun in the palace than it would have been as a Hebrew slave!

Meanwhile, the Hebrew slaves were forced to work hard. Every day they sweated under the hot Egyptian sun, planting crops, building statues, and making bricks out of mud and straw.

One day, when Moses was grown up, he discovered that he was a Hebrew. He set off to visit his real family who lived in a part of Egypt called Goshen. While he watched them making mud bricks, he saw an Egyptian man beating a Hebrew slave.

Moses' heart was filled with anger. "How dare you hit that slave!" he shouted. Moses killed the Egyptian and buried his body in the sand. The next day, Moses went out and saw two Hebrew men fighting each other. "Why are you hitting your friend?" he asked one of the men. "Who are you to tell me what to do?" the man answered. "Will you kill me like you killed that Egyptian?"

Moses' heart pounded with fear. Who else knew he had killed an Egyptian?

When Pharaoh heard what Moses had done, he said, "Find him and kill him!" Moses knew he was in trouble. He fled to a land called Midian, far away from Pharaoh's palace.

Moses sat on the edge of a well in Midian, staring grimly into the distance. *I'm in big trouble*, he thought. *There's no way I can ever go back to Egypt.* Just then the seven daughters of Jethro, a Midianite priest, came to fetch water for their father's sheep. A gang of shepherds tried to scare them, but Moses leapt up and chased them away.

When Jethro heard how Moses had protected his daughters, he invited Moses home to eat with them. "Moses, you have done a great thing for this family," said Jethro. "I will give you my eldest daughter Zipporah to marry!"

Zipporah's sisters clapped their hands. They were happy their sister was getting married. They gathered together and prepared for the wedding.

Did you know?

The land of Midian was located in what is now modern-day Saudi Arabia.

That week the village buzzed with excitement. Zipporah was getting married! Jethro invited all his friends and neighbors to the wedding ceremony. Everyone sang and danced, and had a party that lasted many days and many nights. And from that time on, Moses and Zipporah lived together with Jethro's family.

Each morning, Moses took Jethro's sheep and goats into the wilderness to graze. This wasn't the life Moses had planned, but forty years in the desert gave him lots of time to spend with God. He had grown up like a prince in Pharaoh's palace, and now he was a shepherd in the desert. *I live in the middle of nowhere,* thought Moses. *What is God up to?*

Back in Egypt, things were getting worse for the Hebrew people. But God hadn't forgotten His promise to Abraham, Isaac, and Jacob. He saw how hard the Hebrews worked, and He knew just what to do to set them free.

One day, near a mountain called Sinai, Moses noticed a bush that was on fire yet was not burning up. "That's pretty strange," said Moses. "I better take a closer look." To his surprise, God spoke to him from out of the bush.

"Moses, do not come any closer. You are standing on holy ground. I am the God of Abraham, Isaac, and Jacob." Moses' knees began to tremble. He tore off his sandals and covered his face with his hands.

God continued. "I've seen how badly My people are being treated in Egypt. Go to Pharaoh and tell him to let My people go." Moses wasn't sure if he liked that idea very much. "Why are You sending me?" he asked. "I'm a nobody and a wanted man. Pharaoh won't believe a word I say!"

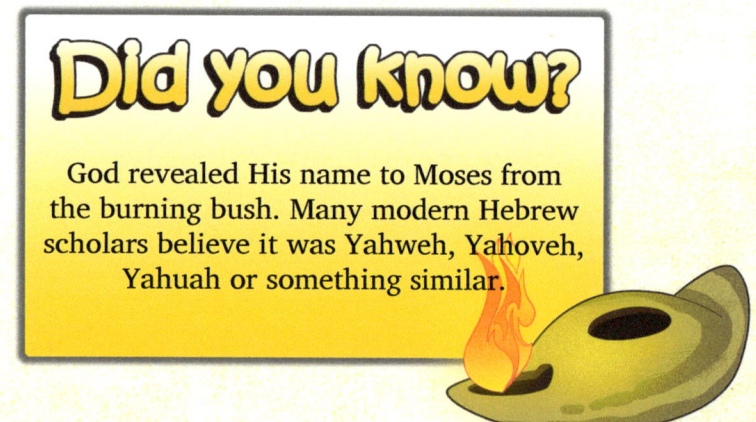

Did you know?

God revealed His name to Moses from the burning bush. Many modern Hebrew scholars believe it was Yahweh, Yahoveh, Yahuah or something similar.

"Listen to Me," said God. "You have nothing to fear. I am going to punish the Egyptians, but I will protect My people. When you've led them out of Egypt, come back and worship Me here on this mountain."

So that people would believe Moses, God showed him how to do signs and wonders. "What's that in your hand?" asked God. "Throw it on the ground!" Moses threw the wooden staff on the ground and it turned into a snake. His eyes nearly popped out of his head. He gazed at the wooden staff in amazement.

But Moses was still worried. "I'm a terrible speaker," he said. "Can't You send someone else?" God became angry with Moses. "Don't you have a brother, Aaron? He talks a lot. I will send him with you. He can speak for you and you can speak for Me." Moses sighed and scratched his beard. There was no getting out of the job God had given him.

Moses and his family set out for Egypt. Soon, Moses' brother Aaron came running out to meet them. God had instructed him to join Moses in the desert. Moses told Aaron everything God had said, and showed him the signs he had been commanded to perform. Aaron stared at the wooden staff in disbelief. He could hardly believe his eyes.

After a few months traveling through the desert, the two brothers finally arrived in Egypt. Aaron spoke to the Hebrew leaders and Moses performed the signs for everyone to see. The Hebrews stamped their feet and danced for joy.

The next day Moses and Aaron took the wooden staff and marched up the steps of Pharaoh's palace. Moses wanted Pharaoh to understand God's message, so he let Aaron do all the talking. Aaron took a deep breath and bowed before Pharaoh. "God wants you to let His people go so they can learn His ways and worship Him."

But God hardened Pharaoh's heart and he became very stubborn. "Who's this god of the Hebrews? I don't know him and I'm not letting anyone go. I need them to work for me!" Pharaoh turned to his slavemasters. "Don't give the lazy Hebrews any straw!" he said. "They can get it themselves. But they must still make the same number of bricks as before."

The Hebrew slaves became angry with Moses. They gathered around him, shaking their fists. "Thanks to you, Pharaoh is working us even harder. You've made our lives worse!" Moses sighed and stared at the sky. "God, why have You sent me?" he asked. "Pharaoh is only making things worse. You haven't helped Your people at all!"

"Wait and see," said God. "By the time I have finished with him, Pharaoh will be glad to see My people leave. Now, go and tell Pharaoh to let My people go."

Aaron and Moses stood before Pharaoh again and told him what God had said. Pharaoh covered his ears and laughed. So Aaron raised the staff and turned the water in the Nile to blood. All the fish died and the Egyptians could not drink any water from the river.

Pharaoh was not impressed. "My magicians can do the same thing," he said. He summoned the magicians and they turned the water at the palace to blood. They couldn't match what God had done but it was good enough for Pharaoh.

Then, God caused millions of frogs to hop out of the river. They jumped through people's houses and crept under their beds. And boy, did they stink! The Egyptian magicians also made the frogs appear but they couldn't make them go away. "Moses, make those frogs disappear!" cried Pharaoh. "If you do, I'll let the people go." But when the frogs were all dead, Pharaoh changed his mind. "The slaves must stay in Egypt."

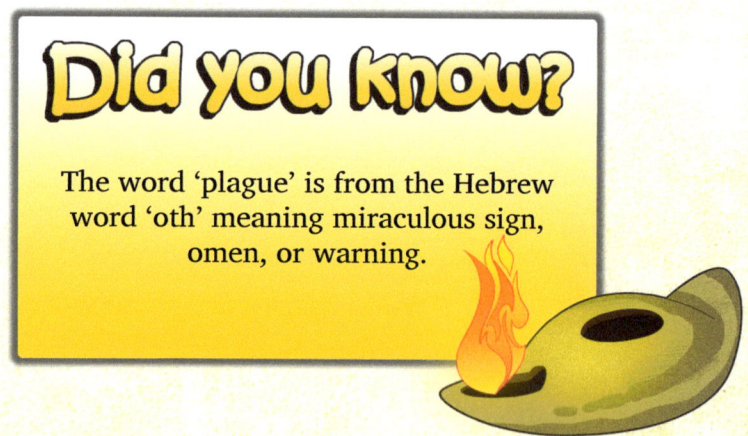

Did you know?

The word 'plague' is from the Hebrew word 'oth' meaning miraculous sign, omen, or warning.

Life was tough for the Egyptians, but Pharaoh's heart remained hard. So God said to Moses, "Tell Aaron to strike the dust on the ground with the staff and I will change the dust to lice." Aaron struck the ground, and lice crawled across the land of Egypt. Pharaoh couldn't stop scratching his head. Those lice were itchy!

The Egyptian magicians tried to use their magic to make the lice appear, but they could not do the same thing. "The Hebrew god must have done this," they told Pharaoh. But Pharaoh did not listen, and he didn't let the Hebrews go.

Next, God sent a swarm of flies over the land, except where the Hebrews lived. The flies buzzed through the palace and around Pharaoh's head. The Egyptians tried to run away from the flies, but the flies chased them everywhere and they couldn't escape. Life was not fun for people in the land of Egypt.

Pharaoh was still stubborn and proud. He refused to let the Hebrews go. So God sent a plague upon the animals of the Egyptians. When the Egyptians woke up the next morning, their donkeys and cattle lay dead on the ground. "How dare none of the Hebrew animals die!" thundered Pharaoh.

Then God said to Moses and Aaron, "Take handfuls of ash from a fireplace and throw them in the air before Pharaoh." Moses did what God asked, and boils appeared on every Egyptian and animal in Egypt. It drove them crazy!

Pharaoh's magicians couldn't even stand up because they were covered in nasty red boils, just like the other Egyptians. They grit their teeth and scratched their legs. "Why can our gods not help us?" God protected His people, and none of the Hebrews in Goshen were covered in boils.

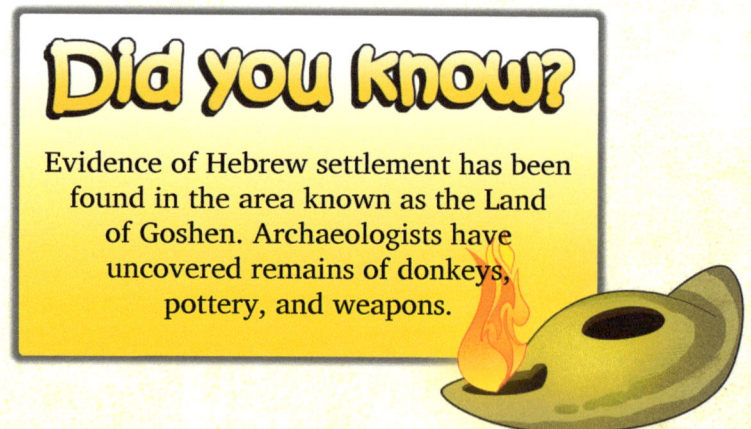

Did you know?

Evidence of Hebrew settlement has been found in the area known as the Land of Goshen. Archaeologists have uncovered remains of donkeys, pottery, and weapons.

Life became harder and harder for the Egyptians. Next, God sent a huge fiery hailstorm. Lightening flashed back and forth, and thunder rumbled through the sky. Hailstones the size of rocks rained down on the Egyptians, and fire from the hail ran along the ground.

But the hail didn't destroy anything in Goshen where the Hebrews lived. It was the strangest hailstorm the Egyptians had ever seen!

Pharaoh clasped his head in his hands and moaned. "Make it stop and I'll let the Hebrew people go." But after the hail and thunder stopped, Pharaoh changed his mind. His heart was still hard, and he didn't let the Hebrews go. Pharaoh's servants begged him to change his mind. "We can't stand these plagues! Can't you see Egypt is being destroyed? Why don't you let the Hebrews go and worship their god?"

Pharaoh thought about what his servants had said. He tried to make a deal with Moses. "Go and worship your god. But only take the men." Moses sighed and shook his head. This was not what God wanted. Moses knew it wouldn't be long before God sent another plague.

Sure enough, God sent a strong wind that blew all day and all night. The next morning the wind brought a swarm of locusts. The locusts flew through Egypt, gobbling all the vegetables and trees, and even the grass. The greedy locusts ate every green thing!

Then, Moses reached out his hand and Egypt turned dark for three days. People couldn't leave their houses because of the darkness. It was as black as midnight. But the Hebrews had light in the land of Goshen. Feeling sorry for himself, Pharaoh sat alone in the dark. "Why are these things happening to me?" But his heart remained hard, and he didn't let the Hebrews go.

Finally, God had had enough of Pharaoh's stubborn behavior. He said to Moses, "I will bring one last plague. At midnight I will kill all the first-born children and animals of Egypt. No one will escape. But if the Hebrew people do what I say, I will spare them. After this, Pharaoh will let them go."

That night, God commanded a sign made from the blood of a lamb be put on the sides of the door and over the doorpost of the Hebrews' homes. This sign would be for their protection. This blood would save them from God's final plague. Little did they know that this sign pointed to their future Messiah.

Just before midnight a cold mist crept through the homes of the Egyptians. Every first-born male died, just as God had warned. But the lamb's blood protected the Hebrews who had listened to God's instructions.

Did you know?

Yeshua was crucified on Passover. The blood placed on the Hebrews' doorposts foreshadowed the blood that would represent His sacrifice for mankind.

Pharaoh was a broken man. He called Moses and Aaron before him. "Get out of here and take the Hebrew people with you. Make sure they take all their belongings. I never want to see them again." Moses patted Aaron on the back. "God has given us a great victory!" he said.

Quickly, the Hebrews gathered their unbaked bread and possessions together. "Give us your gold and silver jewelry," they said to the Egyptians. The Egyptians couldn't wait for the Hebrews to leave. They ripped off their jewelry and flung it at the Hebrews. "We're sick of your god and His plagues. Just leave us for good!"

Filled with excitement, the Hebrews and their friends followed Moses away from Goshen into the wilderness. It had been a long and difficult time, but now their painful suffering was over. "God has delivered us from Pharaoh," the people sang. "Finally, we are free!"

THE END

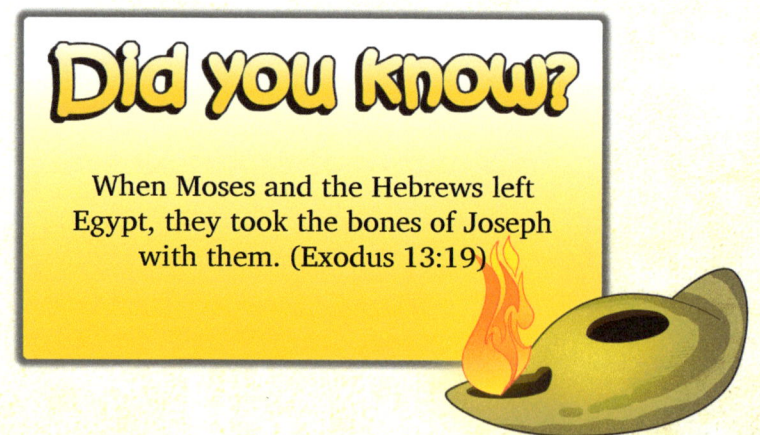

Did you know?

When Moses and the Hebrews left Egypt, they took the bones of Joseph with them. (Exodus 13:19)

TEST YOUR KNOWLEDGE!
(Match the question with the answer at the bottom of the page)

QUESTIONS

What was the first plague? ....

Which plagues did the Egyptian magicians copy? ....

What was the fourth plague? ....

Ashes were used in which plague? ....

Which book of the Bible mentions the plagues? ....

What was the last plague? ....

How many plagues did God send on Egypt? ....

Who hardened Pharaoh's heart after the plague of locusts? ....

What did God tell the Hebrews to do to avoid the final plague? ....

Whose bones did Moses take with him when he left Egypt? ....

ANSWERS

1. Water turns into blood
2. Frogs, and turning water into blood
3. Flies
4. Boils
5. Exodus
6. Death of the firstborn
7. Ten
8. God
9. Mark their doorposts with lamb's blood
10. Joseph (Exodus 13:19)

Bible Pathway Adventures®

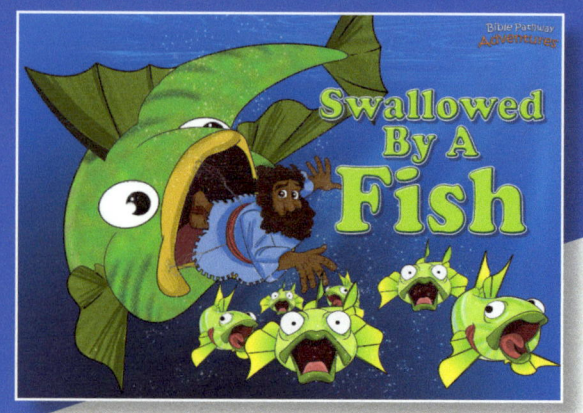

Birth of the King
Betrayal of the King
The Risen King
Swallowed by a Fish
The Chosen Bride
Saved by a Donkey
Thrown to the Lions
Facing the Giant
Samson Mighty Warrior
Sold into Slavery
The Great Flood
Shipwrecked!
The Exodus

Discover more Bible Pathway Adventures' Bible stories!

Check out Bible Pathway Adventures' Activity Books

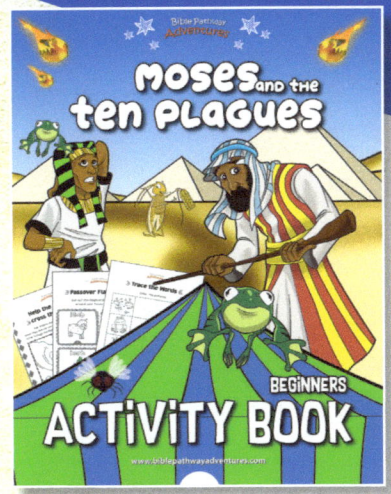
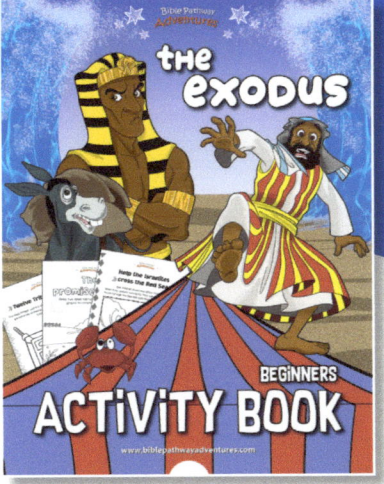
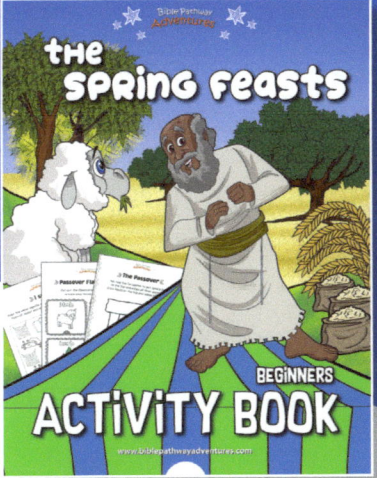
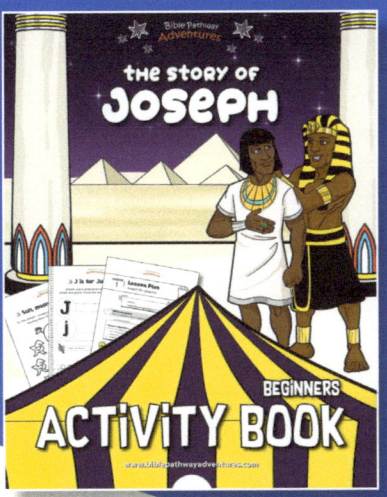
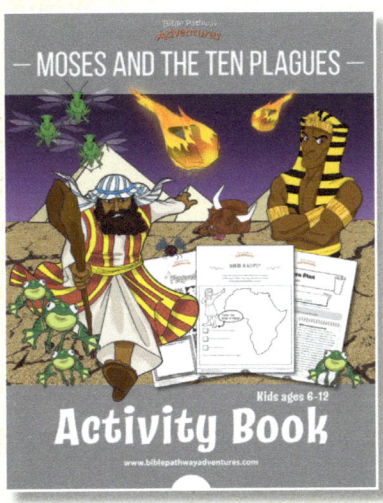
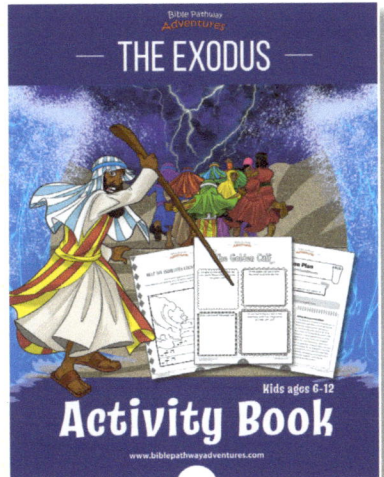
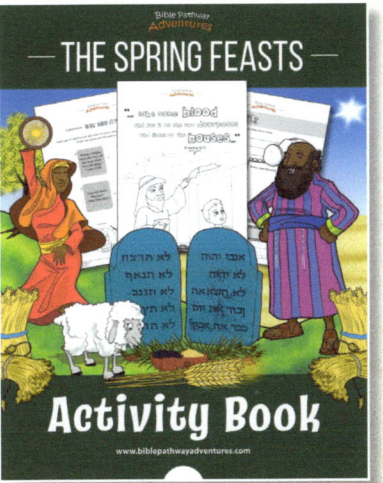
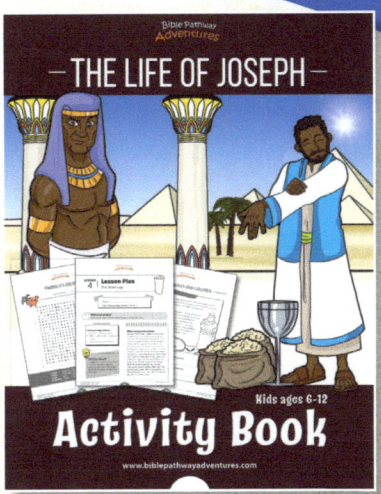

GO TO
www.biblepathwayadventures.com